INTRODUCTION

Welcome to the workbook!

I have created this as a resource for clients, readers of my book and newly-promoted senior managers who are looking to move past feelings of overwhelm and any concerns about their ability to perform in their new role.

The workbook is 100% new material not contained in my book and so is a valuable addition that will walk you through the five principles that the most effective leaders pay attention to.

 Building strong Alliances with key people

 Developing authentic Confidence in your abilities

 Creating Order to your workflow

 Gaining clear Direction both personally and professionally

 Nourishing your Energy levels so you inspire others

The five principles combine to create the A-CODE and together ensure that you are operating at the top of your game.

You can work through this book in the order that the exercises are presented or you can pick the topic that is most relevant for you right now. Each section is a stand-alone section but one or two of them do refer to, or are informed by, exercises in other sections.

Thank you for purchasing this workbook. A great deal of thought and effort has gone into making it and I sincerely hope that it is a useful resource for you.

It is very much a work in progress so please do get in touch and tell me how you got on. If you have positive things to say, please leave me a review on Amazon. If there are things that need further clarification or could make the workbook better for you then please do get in touch and I will integrate your suggestions in the next edition.

You can reach me at any time on workbook@ben-green.co.uk

Wishing you great success and fulfilment in your new role!

Best wishes

Ben

LEAD WITH CONFIDENCE

THE WORKBOOK

ALLIANCES

ALLIANCES

The first step of the A-CODE is to consider the people around you who will help you be effective in your new role. To stand out as an effective leader you will want to develop and strengthen your relationships with these key people.

The 5 steps to creating alliances that will make you successful in your new role are:
1. Audit Current Relationships
2. Identify New Connections
3. Strengthen Key Alliances
4. Set Up Relationship Rhythms
5. Raise Your Profile

The following pages of the workbook contain exercises that will walk you through these steps and leave you with a concrete plan for tackling this area of your leadership journey.

1. AUDIT CURRENT RELATIONSHIPS

The first thing we need to do is take a look at the work relationships that you already have. We need to look for people close to you in the organisation as well as people who are further away from you. This worksheet will help guide you through this.

In the left hand column put the names of people at various levels inside your organisation as well as outside the organisation. Once you have written all the names, rate the strength and quality of the relationship that you have with that person (0 = They barely know who you are and 10 = You would do anything for each other).

Now consider what score you would like this relationship to have and enter a number in the next column.

Once you have written a score for each person, consider what you notice. Are there any lessons you can learn from this audit?

SENIOR PEOPLE	CURRENT SCORE	DESIRED SCORE	ACTION
YOUR BOSS			
PEERS/COLLEAGUES			

ALLIANCES

TEAM/DIRECT REPORTS	CURRENT SCORE	DESIRED SCORE	ACTION

INTERNAL INFLUENCERS

INDUSTRY THOUGHT-LEADERS

ALLIANCES

2. CREATE NEW CONNECTIONS

In addition to strengthening the existing relationships that you have it is also important to think about expanding your network. In this step, use the table below to identify 5-7 people who you would like to connect with. These can be people inside your organisation or they can be contacts at partner organisations, suppliers, clients or customers.

These should be people who you admire or who are influencers within your industry or are able to expand your awareness of your industry in some way.

Write your list of names in the table below and for each one, think of a way that you could connect with them that is going to make them want to have a conversation with you. In a busy world, if you are going to connect with them you need to give them a compelling reason why it is worth their time to do so. You might like to think of this as a short pitch that helps sell them on the idea of getting to know you. Add this to the table below.

Consider if there is any preparatory research or other work you need to do before connecting with this person. Put this information in the Actions column and schedule it in your calendar.

NEW CONNECTION	PITCH	ACTIONS

ALLIANCES

3. STRENGTHEN KEY ALLIANCES

In this step, we are going to combine the lists you have made in the previous two steps.

Look over your lists and pick the top 3-5 people who, if you were to strengthen your relationship with them, would make the biggest difference to you, your role or your work. Write their names at the top of the left hand column of the table below.

Below the top 3-5, you can add the names identified in the previous two worksheets (your current relationships as well as the names of people who you would like to connect with).

Next to each person write down an action you could take to strengthen this relationship. Maybe you could set up a one-to-one.....take them to lunch.....Send them an interesting article.....Give them a call and ask how a project is going.....Offer your team to help them in some way.....

Start with the top 3-5 people on the list and take action now.

If now is not an appropriate time then use this time to schedule in your calendar when you are going to take the necessary actions to expand your network and strengthen your key relationships.

As a leader, it is the people you know and your ability to influence that will determine a big part of your success. Any one of these people could be a key factor in your next introduction, next deal, next problem solved, next promotion, next partnership or next level of your development.

Begin to forge stronger professional alliances and expand your network.

NAME OF PERSON	ACTIONS THAT WILL FORGE A STRONGER ALLIANCE

ALLIANCES

NAME OF PERSON	ACTIONS THAT WILL FORGE A STRONGER ALLIANCE

ALLIANCES

4. SET UP RELATIONSHIP RHYTHMS

Now that you have brought your alliances into your awareness and taken action to strengthen your relationships and expand your network, it is time to consider how you will nurture these relationships on an ongoing basis.

A seed that is planted in the earth relies on regular doses of water, nutrients and light. Our alliances are the same and will wither if they are not given similar attention.

In this step, I want you to consider three levels of nourishment:
1. **The Minimum Input** required for this alliance to be maintained at its current level. (For some alliances this might be a 6-monthly catch-up, for others it might be a daily progress report.)
2. **Behaviours That Will Harm** this particular relationship. (This might be something like forgetting to communicate your actions to someone or not seeking their input on a decision that might affect them or their team.)
3. **Unexpected Contributions** that you could make to wow and delight the other person, and raise their opinion and respect for you. (For example, this might be acknowledging them publicly for a piece of work or it might be sending them a book you thought they'd like to read)

Go ahead and put your ideas in the table below:

PERSON	MINIMUM INPUT	HARMFUL BEHAVIOUR	UNEXPECTED CONTRIBUTION

Now that you have this information about each key relationship, get your calendar and:
1. Schedule in the minimum requirements with reminders
2. Schedule timely reminders to make an unexpected contribution to this relationship

This will ensure that you pay attention to the health of your alliances and are investing in strengthening them on an ongoing basis.

ALLIANCES

5. RAISE YOUR PROFILE

The fifth and final step in strengthening your alliances is all about the relationships that you have with people who you haven't even met yet. These are people who hear about you or your work. It is about your reputation. When you get this handled correctly you will find more and more people wanting to connect with you. This is about becoming a Key Person of Influence in your industry or area of expertise. Once you have created a solid network of strong alliances with key people, this step is about building your brand so that you have a wider impact and stand out as highly credible as a leader in your field.

This may be a step that you return to after you have gone through the rest of the A-CODE. To really have an impact in this area it is best to own the concepts of Confidence, Order, Direction and Energy.

The purpose of this worksheet is simply to raise your awareness and encourage you to dream a little about what this could look like for you[1].

So to get started, notice today's date and write it down but add 3 years on so the date that you write down is in the future.
___/_____/ 20___

Now, looking ahead to that date, where would you like to be in terms of your career, your reputation and your profile?

_____

_____

_____

What would you like to be known for? What impact will you be having in the world?

_____

_____

_____

Who would you like to have in your network? Who would you like to have on your team? Who would you like to be calling you and asking for your advice?

_____

_____

_____

Just for a moment, imagine what it would be like to have achieved that level of credibility in your industry. Imagine the difference it would make to you personally and professionally.

It is possible. There is a route for you to get there and the first step is to dream it. We will develop this further when we get to the DIRECTION section of this workbook.

---

[1] For a deep dive into this topic I highly recommend the book *Become a Key Person of Influence – The 5 Step Sequence to becoming the most highly valued and highly paid people in your industry* by Daniel Priestley.

CONFIDENCE

CONFIDENCE

The second key to the A-CODE is the whole area of confidence. It is an issue that impacts people at all levels but it can be a particularly large block to the effectiveness of newly-promoted senior managers.

I believe there is great power at the intersection of talent and confidence. You are obviously talented. Your seniority is evidence of your abilities. Now it's time to align your confidence so you can tap into this power and really stand out in your new role.
The 5 steps to building lasting confidence in your new role are:

1. Partition your confidence requirements
2. Prioritise the most important areas to tackle
3. Prepare a game plan for maximum confidence
4. Practise feeling confident
5. Progress to the next level

The following pages of the workbook contain exercises that will walk you through these steps until you have a concrete plan for tackling this area of your leadership journey.

1. PARTITION YOUR CONFIDENCE REQUIREMENTS

Every client I have ever discussed issues of confidence with has some areas of life where they feel less confident and some areas where they feel more confident.

The first thing we need to do is identify what these different areas are for you. Let's start with those areas or activities where you are confident. Use the table below to list five things that you do with ease and confidence. It doesn't have to be anything major; just activities where you feel confident and which you may even enjoy. Include one or two activities that you do confidently that others might be uncertain or nervous about.

Once you have your list of confident activities, spend a moment reflecting on how you built confidence in these areas. Consider how you maintain your confidence levels. What do you do? What do you pay attention to? What do you not pay attention to? What do you say to yourself?

Doing this will give you an idea of how you "do" confidence.

Next, it's time to list out those areas of your professional life where you struggle with confidence, where you experience anxiety, nervousness, worry or fear.

Be as specific as possible. Don't list "Giving presentations", instead write "Presenting to the Board when more than 8 people are in the room and Mr X is in a bad mood". It is crucial that you identify in as much detail as possible the specific circumstances where you feel a lack of confidence and would like to improve it.

CONFIDENCE

ACTIVITIES I FEEL CONFIDENT DOING	ACTIVITIES WHERE I'M NOT CONFIDENT

Looking at these two lists, do you see any themes?

_____

_____

Are there any surprises?

_____

_____

Imagine for a moment what it would do for you, your results, your personal impact and your career if you felt the same way about the activities in the right hand column as you do about the activities in the left hand column. What difference would that make?

_____

_____

CONFIDENCE

In the previous step, you identified those activities that you feel confident about and those that you are less confident about. Now, we are going to drill a little deeper to find out which area is the highest priority for us to build confidence levels.

Next to each activity that you identified on the previous worksheet, write a number from 0 - 10 that describes your current level of confidence. 0 = absolutely no confidence and 10 = supremely confident/as confident as you could possibly be.

What do you notice about the activities on the left hand side of the table?

_____

How do they compare to the numbers on the right hand side of the table?

_____

Does anything jump out at you? Does it reveal anything helpful?

_____

Looking at the table on the previous worksheet identify the 3 activities that, if you were to increase your confidence, would make the biggest difference to you, your work, your career. If you want to, consider "What would be an even bigger goal in this area?"

Next, write your three priorities in the Confidence Equalizer below.

For each activity, place a cross on the vertical line to indicate your current confidence level.

For each activity, place a circle on the vertical line to indicate the level that you would like your confidence to be.

You have now prioritised the areas where you are going to build your confidence and given them a current score and a target level that you are aiming for. Before turning to the next worksheet, consider for a moment: what would it take to improve your confidence level by one or two points? What would it take to reach your target level?

Consider these questions for each of your priority activities and then proceed to the next worksheet.

CONFIDENCE

3. PREPARE A GAME PLAN FOR MAXIMUM CONFIDENCE

You are now clear on the activities and environments where you want to improve your confidence. You have assessed your current confidence level and set a target for building your confidence. It is now time to create a plan that will get you to the level of confidence that you would like.

We are not intending to jump off a cliff but instead we will create a pathway of simple steps that will take us closer to the confidence you want. Use the exercise on the next page by working backwards from the end goal. Start by writing on the top right hand side what your end goal is. Write in as much detail the activity that you would be doing, the impact that you'd be making and the confidence score that you would be feeling.

Then, go one step to the left and ask yourself "What would be something that would be just short of this but would be preparation for reaching the next step?"

Repeat this process, working your way backwards along the path until you get to a point where you feel very confident that you are capable and motivated to take the first step.

Use a fresh activity sheet for each of your three priority areas.

I have created an example version below so you can see how it might look.

END GOAL
Deliver keynote at Industry Conference.
CONFIDENCE LEVEL 10

STEP 4
Facilitate company away-day for audience of 200 people.
CONFIDENCE LEVEL 8

STEP 3
Deliver presentation to regional forum of 50-100 people.
CONFIDENCE LEVEL 7

STEP 2
Take every opportunity to speak/present to groups at work.
CONFIDENCE LEVEL 6

STEP 1
Prepare 5-10 minutes of material and present every week to team.
CONFIDENCE LEVEL 5

You can download blank copies of this worksheet at
www.ben-green.co.uk/confidencerocks

15

CONFIDENCE

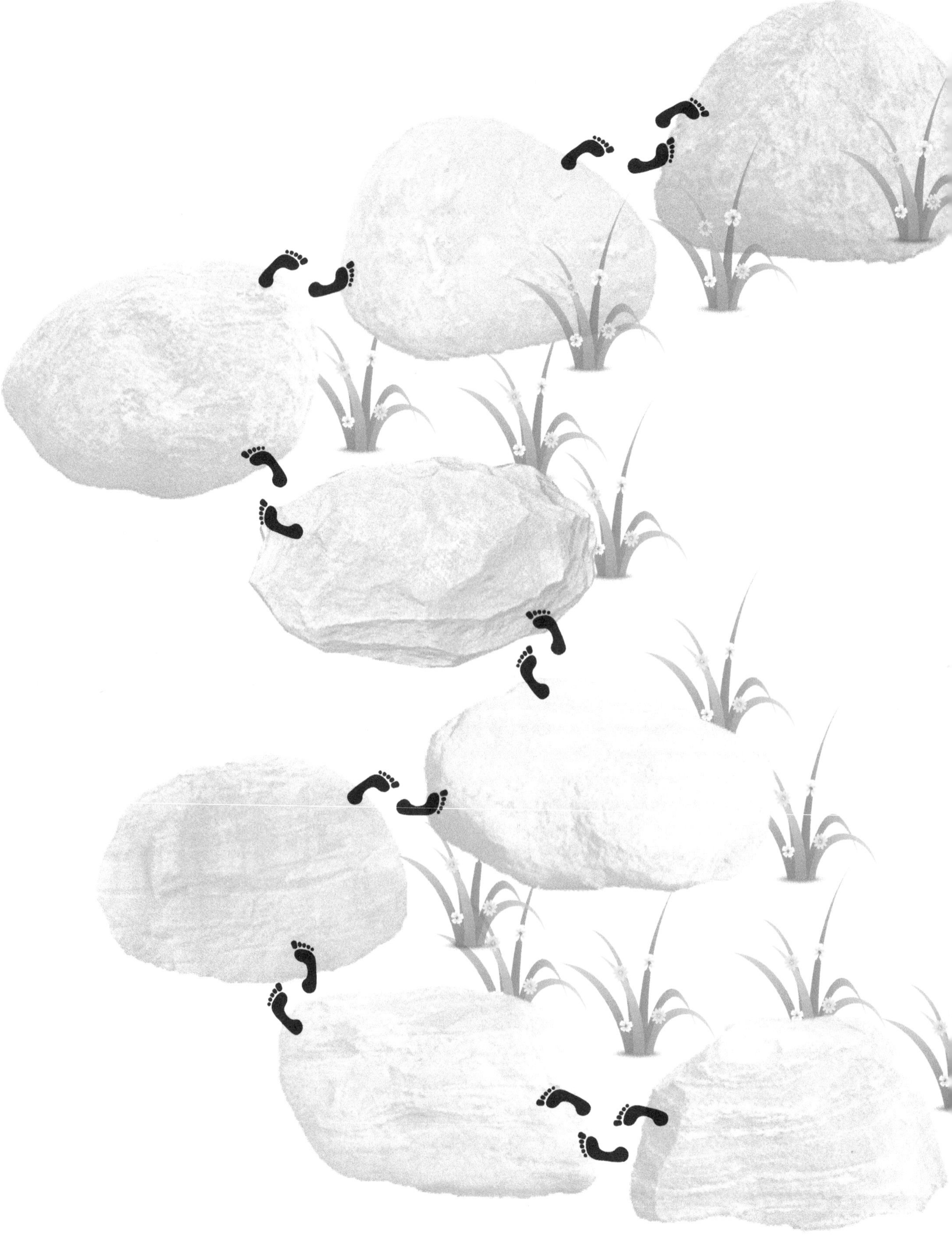

CONFIDENCE

4. PRACTISE FEELING CONFIDENT

Confidence is a feeling that you create in your mind and body. You do it unconsciously most of the time but it is easy to create it consciously whenever you want. If I asked you to make yourself feel sad you could probably find ways to do that. If I asked you to feel happy, there are things that you could do with your face, your posture, your movements and your thoughts that would bring about feelings of happiness.

Referring back to the table on the first confidence worksheet, look over the list on the left-hand side containing the activities that you feel confident doing. Imagine doing one of those activities as vividly as you can. See what you see, hear what you hear and feel what you feel when you are engaged in that activity that you feel confident about. Notice how you breathe, notice how you hold your posture and how you move. Notice what you say to yourself as you're doing it and even the tone of voice that you use to say it. Notice what you focus on.

Now, could you do all of those same things right now and create those same feelings of confidence? Give it a go right now. Go on...this is a workbook so you you're going to have to engage with it to get the benefit. Do all of those same things for a minute or two. Stand or sit or move the way that you move. Think the same thoughts. Breathe in the same way and speak with the same voice.

After a minute or so of this notice the difference in how you feel.

Feeling confident is a skill that you can practise. If you want to get good at feeling confident then take every opportunity you can to develop your confidence muscle by practising feeling confident. When you walk, walk confidently. When you sit, sit in a confident way. When you talk, do so with confidence. Practise, practise, practise.

Refer to the Confidence Equaliser on page 14 and transfer your three priority areas into the first column on page 18. Now refer to the Confidence Rocks worksheet where you came up with a game plan for building your confidence. If you were to watch a film of yourself performing this activity confidently and competently, what would you look like? How would you sit/stand/move/breathe? How would you sound? What would your face look like?

Now, become a method actor. Recreate that movie right now. Move, breathe, talk and do exactly what you were doing in that movie and do it all with confidence.

How do you feel?

Complete the table on page 18 for each of your priorities and schedule a time to practise feeling this way for as long as you can. A minute or two, or five minutes a day, is enough to make a difference. You can either use your phone to schedule a regular reminder or use an event as a trigger to practise. If you sometimes find yourself worrying about things, use that as your trigger to just practise feeling confident. The more you can train your mind to take control of your nervous system and create empowering confident feelings in your body, the stronger you will get at this and the more inspiring you will be as a leader.

This level of emotional intelligence is probably the most important skill that you can develop as a leader.

CONFIDENCE

PRIORITY	ACTIVITY	WHAT I DO TO CREATE FEELINGS OF CONFIDENCE IN MY BODY IS…
1		
2		
3		

CONFIDENCE

The feeling of confidence stems from our personal belief about what we are capable of. When we feel that we can do something well then we experience the feeling of confidence. Any activities or events that we believe we can do well lay within a psychological area known as our Comfort Zone.

Some people say that life begins at the edge of your comfort zone. This is the space where you are facing your fears and developing your abilities and gaining new experiences that fuel your growth as a person.

When you do the exercise and activities outlined in this workbook you will have started to expand your comfort zone. You will feel confident in more areas than you did previously.

You identified these areas because of the worry or nervousness that you felt about certain activities, events or situations.

In this fifth step we are going to consider how you can progress to the next level in your career, your confidence and your contribution. We are going to do this, not by considering what we are not confident about but by looking at what we would like to do and how we would like to grow.

We do this by simply asking the following question over and over again:

"If there were no limits, what would I aim for?"

Pick one area of your professional work and ask that question until you run out of answers and then move on to another area. When you have considered all of the different areas of your role, ask the question of your role as a whole.

"If there were no limits, what would I aim for?"

Consider your career.

I also recommend doing this for every area of your life (e.g. Relationships, Family, Finances, Health, Hobbies etc.).

Use the table below to record your answers and by the end of this exercise I guarantee that you will be feeling energised and inspired about what's possible for you. Dreaming a bigger dream and working to make it a reality is what leadership is all about.

	"IF THERE WERE NO LIMITS, WHAT WOULD I AIM FOR?"
PROFESSIONAL ACTIVITY 1:	
PROFESSIONAL ACTIVITY 2:	

CONFIDENCE

	"IF THERE WERE NO LIMITS, WHAT WOULD I AIM FOR?"
PROFESSIONAL ACTIVITY 3:	
PROFESSIONAL ACTIVITY 4:	
PROFESSIONAL ACTIVITY 5:	
MY ROLE:	
MY CAREER:	
PROFESSIONAL RELATIONSHIPS :	
PERSONAL RELATIONSHIPS:	
FAMILY:	

CONFIDENCE

	"IF THERE WERE NO LIMITS, WHAT WOULD I AIM FOR?"
FINANCES:	
HEALTH:	
HOBBIES:	

We will refer back to this activity and go into more depth when we reach the worksheet in the fourth step of the A-CODE.

You have reached the end of the second step in the A-CODE and you should now have a plan for building your confidence in the areas that are most important to you and your success in the new role. One of my favourite things about being a coach is seeing people transform this area so that things that used to bother them or fill them with dread become easy and even enjoyable. You now have a road map to do this for yourself but even better than that you also have a far bigger vision for what you can achieve.

When you're ready, let's progress to the next section of the workbook where we get organised and create a sense of order to our work so that you can achieve all of the things you want to in your new role.

ORDER

ORDER

The third step in the A-CODE involves working with your ability to bring order to the chaos of life. There are so many different "moving parts" in a senior role that keeping on top of things can sometimes feel like wrestling an octopus. The following five exercise will help you to get a grip on it all, to get organised and to bring order to your world.

In this section of the workbook we will:

1. Audit the Mess
2. Assess and Adjust your Attitude
3. Approach Things Differently
4. Organise a System
5. Accept Chaos

The following pages of the workbook contain exercises that will walk you through these steps and help you to get organised and maintain an effective level of order.

1. AUDIT THE MESS

This step is about identifying where you are experiencing problems or challenges when it comes to getting organised. It is about scanning the environment of your role and noticing where the messiest parts are.

A messy house would have piles of junk laying around, kitchen equipment that doesn't work, doors with squeaky hinges and mould shower curtains. It would not be a pleasant, efficient nor optimum living environment.

In the world of work, I use the word "mess" to refer to electronic, virtual, psychological and real-world mess. Things that slow us down or contribute to a less than optimum working environment.

The most common sources of "mess" identified by senior executives are:

• Emails (hundreds of unread conversations)
• Phone calls (interruptions and unanswered voicemails)
• Paperwork (stacks of reports and reading materials)
• Meetings (requests to attend and need for preparation)
• Time-keeping (managing a diary, finishing on time and getting to places on time)
• Deadlines (pressure to meet deadlines, missing deadlines or relying on others who are unreliable)

Does any of this sound familiar?

ORDER

In this step, I'd like you to take a few minutes to scan your work environment and audit the reality for you. The table on the following page will guide you through the process.

For each work area, describe your current situation. Make a note of the things that are already working well as well as the things that frustrate you or that could be improved.

Next, think about what this work area would be like if it was organised in a way that would optimise your performance. Describe what that would be like.

Now, compared to the ideal ten out of ten environment, how does your current situation compare? Give it a benchmark score out of ten.

This audit is an important first step. In the following worksheets we will use this audit as the starting point for getting organised.

WORK AREA	DESCRIBE THE CURRENT SITUATION	DESCRIBE YOUR IDEAL SITUATION I.E. 10/10	SCORE YOUR CURRENT SITUATION
Emails			
Phone Calls			
Paperwork			
Meetings			
Time-Keeping			
Deadlines			

ORDER

Having conducted an audit of your external environment, it is now time to consider your internal environment. This step is about assessing your beliefs and values around tidiness, order and being an organised person.

Often our external environment is a reflection of our internal belief structure. Any attempts to clean up on the outside are a waste of energy until we create an alignment with our personal values in this area.

For example, if someone holds the belief that:
- "I'm a creative and mess is part of the creative process" or
- "Tidy people are boring" or
- "I have more important work to do than spending time getting organised"

then they will struggle to create and maintain an ordered environment because the activity of being organised does not fit with their personal beliefs.

In this step we are going to assess your attitude towards getting organised and creating order in your working environment. If necessary, you will identify ways that you can adjust your attitude to one that aligns your personal values with your professional aspirations.

Use the following exercise to discover any internal hurdles that may be preventing you from getting a grip on this area of your leadership skillset.

1. Complete the following sentences as many times as you can and write your answers on the lines below:

Tidy people are: _____

_____

_____

Being organised means: _____

_____

_____

2. On the following scale, make a cross that indicates how organised a person you are[1]:

Very
Disorganised _____ Very
Organised

On the same scale draw a circle that indicates how organised a person you would like to be.

---

[1] It can be an interesting exercise to draw this scale and ask others you work with to score you just to see if your perception and your colleagues' perception align.

ORDER

3. Use the table below to record your thoughts about the following:

If I was to become as organised as I would like to be it would have the following impact on:

	POSITIVE	NEGATIVE
Me		
My Work		
My Results		
My Colleagues		
Other Areas		

Once you have completed this table, look at the negative column and for each thing that you have written down, ask yourself, "Is this true or is this just a faulty belief I picked up somewhere?"

Cross off or delete any of these faulty disempowering beliefs.

Now look at the positive column. Read through all of the positive differences that you will make to your life when you become a more organised person. This list needs to inspire you enough that it feels worthwhile taking action on a daily basis to be organised and reap the rewards listed in the positive column. The more benefits you can see, the more likely you are to succeed at this leadership skill.

4. So far we have been assessing what you believe already. It is now time to design some new beliefs that will support you to make the changes that you want. You can use your own creativity to come up with these and you could also speak to others who are particularly good at this skill. Tell them that you've noticed that they are very organised or very good at something, e.g. handling email and ask them what they believe about this.

What would be some useful beliefs that you could adopt in this area? What beliefs could you adopt that would make this a fun, enjoyable part of your role?

ORDER

I believe that:

-
-
-
-
-
-
-
-

Now, write these beliefs somewhere where you are going to be reminded of them on a daily basis, perhaps in your calendar's reminder system or in a phone app like "Me But Better".

Before we go on

Assessing and adjusting your attitude in this way shows a high level of emotional intelligence. The ability to be flexible and to be intelligent enough to design beliefs that support your professional skills development are high order skills.

The work that you do on yourself in this exercise is the key to making effective and lasting changes.

In the next worksheet we are going to identify ways that you can start approaching your work differently. This is where you will be testing, improving and strengthening your empowering beliefs so that they support your new behaviours.

In some ways this might be a stretch outside of your comfort zone.

We get comfortable with familiar ways of doing things.

These habits can become our default.

It is the new beliefs that you have developed that will make your new approach a logical and rewarding way of doing things and when you get your house in order you will definitely stand out as an effective leader.

ORDER

3. APPROACH THINGS DIFFERENTLY

Now that you have audited the mess and taken steps to adjust your attitude, we are going to consider how you would like to approach things differently. In other words, what are you going to do that will create and maintain order in your professional life?

As we get ready to take this next step, it is important that you already have some ideas of the kinds of changes you would like to make.

If you've read my book or done some research on how to get organised at work, handle emails, meetings, paperwork etc. then you probably have some ideas about what you could and would like to change about the way you currently operate.

If you are not sure about what changes to make then I suggest you do some research, read my book or use this as a topic of discussion between you and your coach.

In this step you will need to refer to the table on page 25 and the audit that you completed.

Read the description of your optimum working environment - the ten out of ten scenario where you are operating in an ordered, efficient and effective manner.

Notice the score that you gave for this area currently.

Consider what you can do to improve this score and raise it one point closer to the ideal scenario.

Consider what it would take to improve this score all the way to ten, the ideal scenario.

Now, using the table on the next page develop your action plan.

Who do you need to communicate with?

What changes do you need to make?

What will you do differently?

How can you start today ?

The First Step

Getting order to our working life is about freeing up time so that you can focus on the most important things where you add the most value...and yet, getting organised takes a significant investment of our time.

This is one of the reasons why people muddle on. Getting organised is seldom an urgent task and so other activities take priority. We get by. We cope with the disorder.

When we start to approach things differently we have to do it with a beginners' mind. We have to understand that things might slow down at first, that we may need to take a step backwards in order to take a leap forwards.

ORDER

WORK AREA	FIRST STEPS THAT WILL IMPROVE THINGS IMMEDIATELY	FULL PLAN THAT WILL FULLY OPTIMISE YOUR WORKING ENVIRONMENT
Emails	<li></li><li></li><li></li>	<li></li><li></li><li></li>
Phone Calls	<li></li><li></li><li></li>	<li></li><li></li><li></li>
Paperwork	<li></li><li></li><li></li>	<li></li><li></li><li></li>
Meetings	<li></li><li></li><li></li>	<li></li><li></li><li></li>
Time-Keeping	<li></li><li></li><li></li>	<li></li><li></li><li></li>
Deadlines	<li></li><li></li><li></li>	<li></li><li></li><li></li>
	<li></li><li></li><li></li>	<li></li><li></li><li></li>

ORDER

Let's start by defining the word:

system

1. a set of things working together as parts of a mechanism or an interconnecting network; a complex whole.
2. a set of principles or procedures according to which something is done; an organised scheme or method.

In order to create a system for organising the various aspects of your work we need three things:
1. A set of procedures
2. A list of principles to guide decision making
3. Someone or something to take action in accordance with the principles and procedures. This will be:
   - You
   - Someone else
   - A computer programme

For example, let's consider a system for dealing with phone-calls. We don't want to be interrupted constantly by people ringing us but we do value having spoken conversations with people so we create the following system.

PRINCIPLES	PROCEDURES	ACTION TAKER
Phone calls are unplanned activity and so reduce daily productivity	My phone is switched to silent during working hours.	Me
	My voicemail message informs people that I do not answer unscheduled calls nor do I listen to voicemails. It tells them my PA's landline.	Me / PA
	I do not give people my mobile number, I give them my PA's landline.	Me
	When I call people on my work phone it is set to withhold my number.	Me/My phone
I should always be contactable in case of emergency by my PA	My phone is set so that there is a distinctive ringtone and sound when my PA calls or texts me.	Me/PA/My phone
I value voice conversations	My PA schedules phone conversations with people I value having conversations with. She includes the person's phone number in the appointment and informs the person that I will call them at the scheduled time and it will show as a withheld number.	PA
	When people ask me or email me to discuss something I have a template reply that asks them to book a phone appointment with my PA.	Me/My computer/PA

ORDER

Now, I'm not saying this is the perfect system. You might not think it would work for you but the point is simply to show you an example so that you can design a system that will work for you.

It's your turn.

Use the table to draw up a system for each of your work areas. The aim should be to minimise the input required from you whilst maximising the effectiveness in terms of your results.

Start with the operating principles. These are statements that indicate what you are trying to achieve and the rationale for the procedures. The principles provide a context for understanding why you or someone else should follow the procedures.

The procedures must be clear and specific actions. They can almost be like a computer programme. If X then do Y.

It should also be clear who is responsible for taking the action outlined in the procedures.

Use the tables on the following sheets to draw up systems that will work for you. You might want to just draw up the principles and then pass the sheets to someone else to devise and create the procedures. The most important thing is that everyone involved in the system needs to be made aware of, and consulted about, the principles, procedures and actors.

The system will probably evolve and it is a good idea from time to time to review how well the system is working. I'm not sure that a perfect system exists so avoid the temptation to throw the baby out with the bathwater. The aim is to create a way of working that maximises your effectiveness whilst minimising your input.

EMAILS

PRINCIPLES	PROCEDURES	ACTION TAKER

ORDER

PHONE CALLS

PRINCIPLES	PROCEDURES	ACTION TAKER

ORDER

PAPERWORK

PRINCIPLES	PROCEDURES	ACTION TAKER

ORDER

PRINCIPLES	PROCEDURES	ACTION TAKER

ORDER

TIME-KEEPING

PRINCIPLES	PROCEDURES	ACTION TAKER

ORDER

DEADLINES

PRINCIPLES	PROCEDURES	ACTION TAKER

ORDER

WORK AREA: _____

PRINCIPLES	PROCEDURES	ACTION TAKER

5. ACCEPT CHAOS

It may seem strange that the final worksheet in this chapter about creating order is titled Accept Chaos. The reason for this is because I have seen some people become so obsessive about systems and procedures that they become overly stressed by them. Not only that but they create stress for others and become slaves to the system rather than using the systems to create more freedom for themselves.

In most business operations there is normally a cycle of:

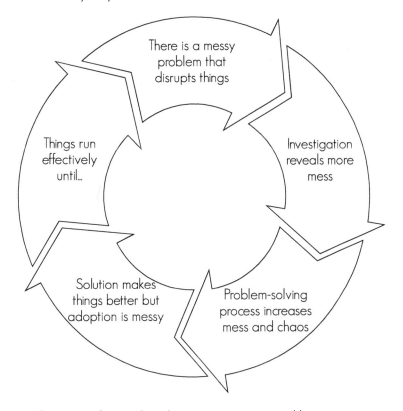

As you can see, there is only a small amount of time when things are running smoothly.

Business is about solving problems more effectively than other organisations.

Being a leader is about using the organisation's resources to solve problems more effectively.

There is a saying that "Every problem contains the seed of its solution" but it is also true that every solution contains the seed of the next problem.

Effective leaders are able to ride wave after wave of problem-solution-problem cycle and use them to carry them through their career rather than smash them to pieces.

Mastering the third step of the A-CODE is an ongoing process and if you cannot accept the chaotic nature of life and of business then your resilience will be tested and ultimately your career will suffer.

The exercise on the next page will not be applicable to everyone but there is always value in reflecting on your own competencies and considering ways you can improve.

ORDER

If you ever feel that things are out of control and this is causing you stress, the following worksheet is designed to ground you and help focus your attention in a way that will be beneficial.

1. What is causing you concern? _____

_____

2. On the scale below put a cross that indicates the level of concern you are feeling:

Not   Complete
Concerned _____ Overwhel

                  Low Level   Very
                  Stress   Worried

On the scale, put a circle to indicate what you consider a healthy level of concern about this issue would be.

3. Have you done everything within your control to solve this? _____

4. Is there anything more that you could do? If so, what? _____

_____

_____

5. How could you surf this better? _____

_____

_____

6. Are you willing to pause and be at peace with the chaos for 1 minute? _____

                                  1 hour?   _____

                                  1 day?   _____

                                  1 week?   _____

7. After the pause, what action will you take? Who will you talk with? What will you do?

_____

_____

_____

_____

DIRECTION

DIRECTION

The fourth step in the A-CODE is about getting very clear on your personal and professional direction so that you can generate outstanding results in your new role but also so you can use this role as a stepping stone to make sure you are having the impact that you want.

In this section of the workbook we will:

1. Reflect on the Journey So Far
2. Reassess Where You Find Yourself Now
3. Raise Your Game
4. Realign Your Daily Actions
5. Regularly Review

The following pages of the workbook contain exercises that will walk you through these steps and help you get crystal clear on your personal and professional mission so you feel excited, contribute more and gain even more fulfilment from your new role.

1. REFLECT ON THE JOURNEY SO FAR

The day to day hustle of corporate life leaves little time for reflection and personal realisation. Often events and decisions are made with little thought to the long-term consequences and we find ourselves in positions where we have strayed from our earlier dreams or career aspirations.

Maybe you are in the role that you always wanted. Maybe you are surprised at just how high you have risen in the organisation. Maybe you feel you are working for a pay cheque rather than fulfilling your life's destiny. Whatever the case is for you, there is benefit to be gained from pausing, taking a look at the current landscape, checking your compass and mapping out the next leg of your journey.

Tell Me About Your Career To Date

A common warm-up question at interview is "Tell me about your career to date..."

This allows the candidate to trot out a well-rehearsed potted history and settle in to the interview process. I'm going to ask you to do something similar but instead of aiming to impress an interview panel you are going to take a good look at the factors that have brought you to your current position.

These factors will probably be deeper and more personal than anything you have shared in an interview. They will help you to see patterns and lead you to a greater self-awareness and understanding that will help you in your current role as well as future decisions.

What Brought You Here Today?

I want you to cast your mind right back to the beginning and think about your early choices around education and/or career choice.

What were your motivations at the time?

What choices were open to you?

DIRECTION

What events or people influenced you?

What decisions did you make and why?

What were your dreams?

Record your answers to the questions in the diagram below.

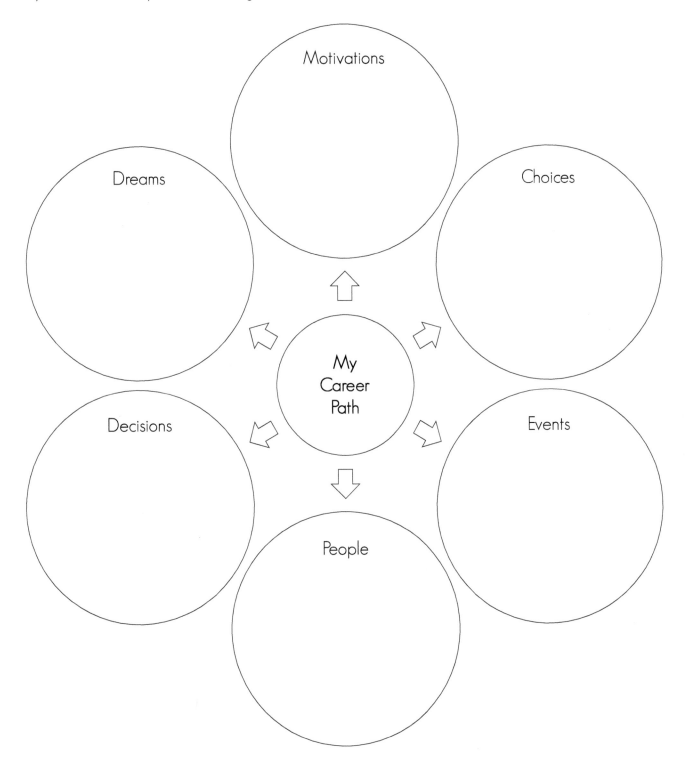

DIRECTION

When you have done that, repeat the process for each major job change or promotion throughout your career. Add your motivations, choices, events, people, decisions and dreams to the diagram so that you build up a picture of your whole career to date.

After you have added your latest promotion to the diagram, take a look at each factor and notice if there are any themes.

What do you notice?

What are the lessons for you?

What are the "takeaways" for you?

Write a quick summary of what you learned from reflecting on your career path in this way: _____

_____

_____

_____

_____

_____

DIRECTION

Having reflected on the journey so far and noticed any themes relating to your career path we will now re-assess where you find yourself. We need to start this personal assessment by defining what success really looks like for you. By reminding yourself of some of your earlier dreams and aspirations you should be in a good position to truthfully define what the ideal position would look like for you.

If you could create a role for yourself that combines your dreams, your natural talents and your motivations to contribute, what would that role look like? You are describing your dream job at the centre of the target below.

Once you have described your ideal role, place an X on the target that indicates where you find yourself now in your current position.

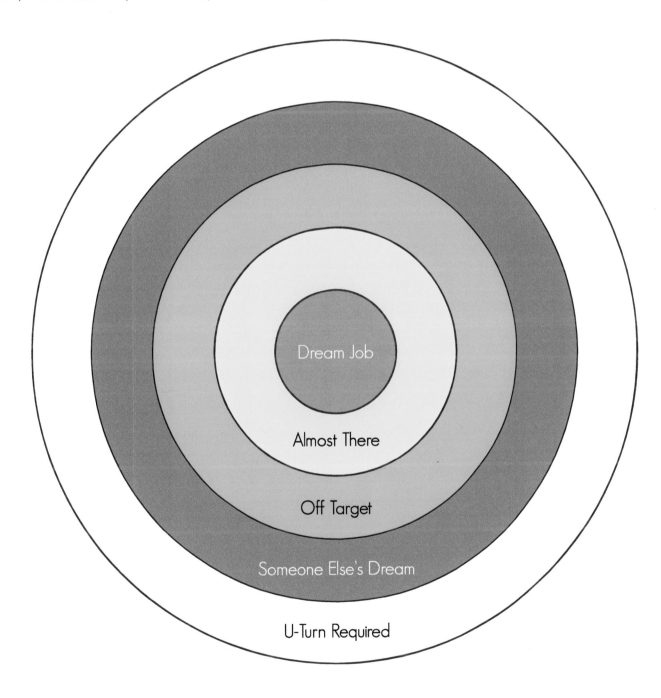

DIRECTION

If you have placed an X in the red or yellow circles, take a moment to acknowledge and congratulate yourself on what you've achieved. It is important to celebrate our successes and this is a big win that only a small proportion of the population achieve. Well done! Have a think about what little tweaks you need to make to stay in this zone and take yourself even closer to the centre.

If you placed an X in the blue circle, then you obviously have more work to do but let's face it you have achieved a level of career success that surpasses many so it should be fairly easy for you to re-aim and use your skills and abilities to hit the dream job. You might want to set some time aside for action planning to get yourself there sooner rather than later or you might want to discuss this with your coach.

If you placed an X in the grey or white circles, then chances are that although you have reached a level of external success you probably are not feeling fulfilled or proud of the work that you are doing. Definitely consider discussing this with your coach as a situation like this needs a bit more input than this workbook is designed to provide.

No matter where you find yourself, use this process of Reassessment as an opportunity to acknowledge, celebrate and enjoy the success that you have accomplished. In the next steps we will Raise Your Game and Realign Your Daily Actions so that at all times you are on the very best path for you.

DIRECTION

It's time to create a higher standard for yourself and raise your game. By making some small changes today and altering our direction of travel by even a few degrees we will plot a course that will take us to a very different destination.

Looking back over your career you probably noticed moments or decisions when you had to raise your game either by learning new skills, taking a risk or accepting greater responsibilities. Often these were decisions taken in the moment, responding to the threats or opportunities of the moment.

Today we are going to plan ahead and start raising our game so that we create the opportunities that you want and maximise your readiness to capitalise on them when they arise.

We are also going to expand your vision of what's possible for you and aim to increase exponentially the results and rewards you receive.

If you refer back to the worksheet on page 19 "Progressing to the next level of Confidence", you'll recall that you considered what would be possible in your career if there were no limits. We're now going to work with this idea so that we can make it happen.

Start by reading through what you wrote on pages 19-21 then return to this page.

What level do you want to play at?

Sometimes my clients struggle to really believe or articulate what could be possible for them if they had no limits so we start with a more manageable thought experiment.

Look at the table on the next page and for each topic consider what would have to happen for you to increase this area by just 10 per cent.

I have put topic headings in the first column but you don't have to limit yourself to these. Cross them out and write your own topics in or add extra topics to the end of the list. I also recommend doing this exercise with other areas of your life. You don't have to just use these great tools to improve your work-life when you can use them to improve your whole life.

DIRECTION

TOPIC	WHAT WOULD HAVE TO HAPPEN FOR YOU TO INCREASE THIS BY JUST 10 PER CENT?
A current project	
An ongoing role-related responsibility	
Your level of fulfilment in the role	
Your level of success in the role	
The contribution you make to your professional community	
Profitability or Savings of your department .	

A 10 per cent improvement is a significant and achievable goal. Small tweaks might be all that is needed to start reaping this kind of positive change but what if we think a bit bigger than this? Repeat this exercise but this time ask what would have to happen for you to double your results in this area?

DIRECTION

TOPIC	WHAT WOULD HAVE TO HAPPEN FOR YOU TO DOUBLE YOUR RESULTS IN THIS AREA?
A current project	
An ongoing role-related responsibility	
Your level of fulfilment in the role	
Your level of success in the role	
The contribution you make to your professional community	
Profitability or Savings of your department	

Imagine having that kind of impact! When you achieve that, would you feel good about it? Do you think you'd stand out as an effective leader? Would your boss be glad that you were promoted or hired into your current role? Well now it's time to expand your thinking into the realm of the greatest leaders of our time. What would have to happen for you to 10X your results in this area? To exponentially increase your results by a factor of ten, what would have to happen?

DIRECTION

TOPIC	WHAT WOULD HAVE TO HAPPEN FOR YOU TO 10X YOUR RESULTS IN THIS AREA?
A current project	
An ongoing role-related responsibility	
Your level of fulfilment in the role	
Your level of success in the role	
The contribution you make to your professional community	
Profitability or Savings of your department	

I told you that this section was about raising your game. You are now thinking at the level that entrepreneurs and CEOs like Steve Jobs, Richard Branson and Bill Gates have always thought at. In the next worksheet we will take these new goals that you have created and start taking action to create massive results in the areas that you feel most inspired by.

DIRECTION

What you do in work each day is a reflection of your thinking up until this point. To raise your game in the ways you have identified in the previous worksheet you will need to re-align these daily actions with your new expanded vision of who you are and what you are here to achieve.

To what level DO you want to play at?

☐ Cruising at current altitude   ☐ Double or nothing

☐ 10% increment   ☐ 10X

To Do or not To Do, that is the question.

There is a well-known story about a conversation that Warren Buffet had with his personal pilot. The story goes that Buffett went up to his pilot named Steve and jokingly said to him: "The fact that you're still working for me tells me I'm not doing my job."

"You should be out going after more of your goals and dreams," Buffett reportedly said.

To help him with that, Buffett asked Steve to list the 25 most important things he wanted to do in his life.

Then Buffett asked that he review each goal and choose the five most crucial ones.

After considering a moment, he drew circles around five fantastic goals, confirming with Buffett that yes, indeed, they were his highest priorities.

And the rest?

"What about these other 20 things on your list that you didn't circle?" Buffett asked. "What is your plan for completing those?"

Steve knew just what to say.

"Well, the top five are my primary focus, but the other 20 come in at a close second," the pilot said. "They are still important, so I'll work on those intermittently as I see fit as I'm getting through my top five. They are not as urgent, but I still plan to give them dedicated effort."

Buffett suddenly turned serious.

"You've got it wrong, Steve," he said. "Everything you didn't circle just became your 'avoid at all cost list.' No matter what, these things get no attention from you until you've succeeded with your top five."

Here, Buffett shows that he doesn't just understand the value of companies, but also the value of time.

Similarly, he once urged Bill Gates to keep his schedule as clear as possible, keeping himself free of the crush of requests that come to a person with the stature of Gates and Buffett.

DIRECTION

"You've gotta keep control of your time," Buffett said, "and you can't unless you say no. You can't let people set your agenda in life[1]."

So, turning to your new ambitions, whether it be to increase by 10 per cent, to double or to 10X your results, you're not going to achieve them by doing the same things you've been doing up until now.

Use the following table to create your high-level To Do and Avoid At All Costs lists.

The To Do list is the daily or weekly activities that will accelerate, fuel or otherwise keep you focussed on and contributing to your new vision.

On your Avoid At All Costs list put those activities that have the potential to draw you off course, to sap your time and drain your energy. They are activities that add nothing to the high-level expanded vision you are creating.

TO DO	AVOID AT ALL COSTS
•	•
•	•
•	•
•	•
•	•
•	•
•	•
•	•

Now it might not be possible to immediately drop all of the activities on your Avoid At All Costs list. Some of them you may need to delegate or get handled in some other way. You should make it a priority to get these off your plate as soon as possible.

At the same time, be wary of new time-suck activities that get thrown your way. Keep in mind that the ability to say "No" to people is a crucial skill that all successful leaders have had to learn.

Whether you like the programme or not, Dragons Den is an excellent illustration of successful entrepreneurs demonstrating this ability. It is a very small percentage of pitches that walk away with funding and that is because the dragons understand that if they say "Yes" to the wrong thing it will cost them time and money that could be invested in the success of their other ventures.

Take a moment to plan and schedule in your diary exactly how and when you will delegate and drop the activities on your Avoid At All Costs list.

Doing this will realign your daily actions in support of your bigger vision.

---

[1] First read on lifehacker.com

DIRECTION

In Chapter Seven of my book there is a template for your Directed Manifesto which includes space for you to outline your vision for your career over the next year, three years and five years. If you have completed your Direction Manifesto you may want to update it to reflect the work you have done here.

Obviously, these will need reviewing regularly. Your five-year vision will probably need updating every few years.

You will probably want to tweak your three-year vision at the end of each year and your vision for this year will need to be completely re-written within twelve months.

Schedule time in your diary to do this.

Of more immediate importance to the achievement of your goals are quarterly, monthly and weekly reviews of the progress you're making towards your vision.

Project by Project – The Chunk Chip Sliver System

As you look at your vision for the year you will be able to identify some key projects that need to be completed to take you closer to the goals for the year. I recommend identifying three projects that can be achieved within a 3-month time-frame.

If you can only identify projects that will take longer than three months, the best thing you can do is divide them into sub-projects of a 3-month timescale. I call these 3-month projects "chunks".

If you can complete three chunks in a quarter that adds up to twelve chunks in a year which is a sizable amount of work. If you tried to achieve anything of that size it would be overwhelming but broken down in this way it becomes very achievable as well as having a weighty satisfaction.

Based on the work you have done in this section and your Direction Manifesto from my book, choose the three most important 3-month chunks of work you will complete this quarter. Enter them into "The Weekly Chip off the Chunk Planner" below by writing a descriptive name for each chunk in the top row of each column. For each Quarterly Chunk write 3 pieces of work that if you completed them this week would chip away at the big quarterly project.

	QUARTERLY CHUNK 1:	QUARTERLY CHUNK 2:	QUARTERLY CHUNK 3:
Weekly Chip #1:			
Weekly Chip #2:			
Weekly Chip #3:			

DIRECTION

For the next thirteen weeks, this table will become your daily and weekly planning tool. On a Friday afternoon, a Sunday evening or a Monday morning look over the previous week's sheet and cross off everything that you got done and then fill out "The Weekly Chip off the Chunk Planner" for the week ahead. The Chip of the Chunk Weekly Planner and Daily Sliver Schedule are available to download at www.ben-green.co.uk/chunks

After a week or two of using this system you will love it because you get way more done and you feel far more satisfaction from the work you accomplish.

Daily Slivers

With the weekly reviews taken care of you will also want to introduce the "The Daily Sliver Schedule" to your routine.

A sliver is an activity or group of activities that take between 1-3 hours to complete. Each Sliver that you complete takes you closer to completing a Weekly Chip and each Chip takes you closer to completing a Quarterly Chunk.

Either at the end of the day or the start of the day you can use the "The Daily Sliver Schedule" to review the work done and plan the next day's work.

You should be able to complete between two and five slivers per day.

TODAY'S SLIVERS	SPECIFIC NEXT ACTION
Sliver 1:	
Sliver 2:	
Sliver 3:	
Sliver 4:	
Sliver 5:	
Captures/Notes:	

Having completed this section of the workbook you should feel very clear on your direction and if you implement the Quarterly Chunk Planning System you will quickly achieve results that will help you stand out as an effective and inspirational leader.

Whilst it is exciting and inspiring to raise your game like this it will require a lot of energy on your part and on your team's part to drive things forward. The final section of the workbook will guide you in creating a high energy lifestyle that supports your career ambitions.